The poetry of Wayne Allen LeVine is the quintessence of quiet passion, purity and a reverence for life and nature. It carries with it a childlike wonder that highlights and heightens the magic of his world to enter the consciousness of his readers. Reading and hearing his poetry is a privilege for those with whom he shares his genius.

> – Louise Cabral,
> author of six novels including A Pageant of Shadows, An Uncommon Bond and Islands of Recall – Writing a Life Story with Guided Imagery

Until now, I have never been a lover of poetry. But at last, Wayne LeVine makes it accessible for me. He touches my heart, and expresses the kind of sentiment which needs to be said about humankind.

> – Donna Theodore,
> concert artist, Broadway and television performer

Being a public speaker and a recording narrator, I too have a love of language, as poet Wayne LeVine obviously does. In his case, it's not the flowery or verbose use of words, but rather the just-right word picture which rings in your heart, reminding you of something lost or something longed for…or something you hold dear. Wayne is a poet for the modern age, with classic foundation.

> – Don Martin,
> Co-founder of PALS, a Creative Arts Ministry

Myths & Artists

P
O
E
M
S

Myths & Artists

POEMS

Wayne Allen LeVine

The Center Press

A Quality Book Publisher

A Quality Book Publisher

Myths and Artists: Poems by Wayne Allen LeVine

Published by The Center Press
P.O. Box 6936
Thousand Oaks, CA 90360

Library of Congress Cataloging-in-Publication Data

LeVine, Wayne Allen, 1955-
Myths and artists : poems / by Wayne Allen LeVine.
p. cm.
ISBN 1-889198-12-9 (pbk. : alk. paper)
1. Artists—Poetry. 2. Mythology—Poetry. I. Title.
PS3612.E928M98 2006
811'.6--dc22
2006011477

Cover Art and Interior Design by Tanya Maibordia
Printed by Media Lithograph

Printed and bound in the United States
10 9 8 7 6 5 4 3 2 1

In honor of the artist that lives in us all,
with the wish to breath beauty into our world.

Contents

Opening Words to the Reader

I hear dogs barking in the background–beyond the tree line standing at the perimeter of my private balcony. Shadows of leaves reaching into openness and sunlight. Potted plants offering shade to a dusty dark green table.

And the romance of my world is all around me…morning doves making their signature sound, while regal pines reflect morning light from their dew covered branches. Then slowly I begin to bring my focus in–from sky to tree line to the wood rail at the edges of my balcony. I bring my awareness in – closer, all the way into my own light, into my own sound, into my own dew-collected glow.

This is my courtship with consciousness–my shinning romance with my own awareness and the making of a mythical life. These are of the essence of my deeper thoughts and fruitful imaginings – the lore of a warrior poet that found peace through artful expression… words and phrases written in the sacred rhythm of an adventurous timekeeper's quest, the unrestrained outpourings of a solar-powered poet in search of his own legacy.

These are the realized dreams of a neglected child who found his own benevolence–alone on a lake, floating in a rowboat, atop warm murky water – a lake wherein seaweed grew wild, and sometime wrapped itself around the wooden oars of a lonely boy searching for himself. These are much more than a faithful collection of memories, though they are partly that. These are some of the discoveries of a willful, open-eyed child, that found courage in artful solitude – the musings of a boy in a rowboat, the dreams procured by a weepy-eyed child, with the heart of a man willing to remember the lavender wings of dragonflies hovering over his head, reflecting sunlight.

And it is the pure aliveness of the many memories such as those, which fuel the spirit of the words that I write now. Those glowing moments of chosen aloneness—the longing for certain selected solitudes, within the majestic spaces of my youth, were the prognostic instances of this radiant awareness that dances within and around me now.

They are as potent today as the dreams, visions and heart-felt desires that I attached to the lavender wings of phosphorescent dragonflies, in order to watch them soar while I floated alone in my rowboat. They are as alive today as the thirsty-green leaves, now growing out of the plentiful branches of my Mimosa tree, that lives just beyond my balcony – the balcony that offers me endless beginnings, in exchange for my willingness to accept them.

These are the soulful footprints of a poetic mountain climber – the ink-stained ropes that could be used to help secure the footing of other courageous climbers, wishing now to find their own way.

> "People say that what we're all seeking is a meaning for life. I don't think that's what we're really seeking. I think that what we're seeking is an experience of being alive, so that our life experiences on the purely physical plane will have resonances within our own innermost being and reality, so that we actually feel the rapture of being alive…"
>
> Joseph Campbell

Poetry permits me to experience my own true aliveness – deeply and fully, compels me to then express some of those resonances within my own innermost being. And it is, I believe, through our own creative, artful and authentic expression, that we are permitted to actually feel the rapture of being alive.

Wayne Allen LeVine

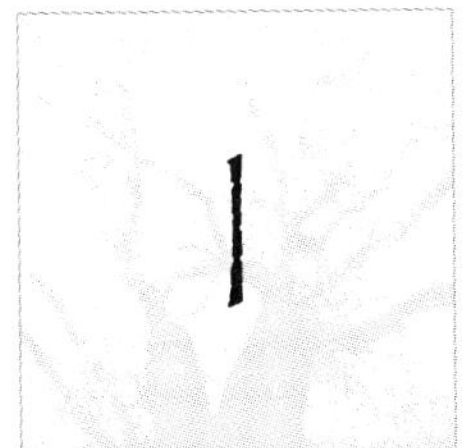

Living in a No Waste World

And it only takes the smallest thing
to draw me in – to bring me in and
give me my beginning. Like a single

drop of coffee, spilling over the edge
of my cup – dripping
through Van Gogh's Starry Night.

Of course, it could be seen as an
over anxious spill – the quick,
unconscious stirring of a
freshly brewed cup of wanted coffee.

Though seen through the eyes of a
poet or painter, it's bound to be seen
as something else. A single drop of coffee,
winding down the side of my porcelain mug,

becomes a Sumatran goddess writhing
in 17th century ecstasy,
on the outskirts of a lively Parisian town.

Or the sacred earth-energy,
held inside a coffee bean, soaring
back to the darkened sky it fell from.

Or the spirit of Vincent Van Gogh
himself, adding the color of coffee to
the stolen image of his own Starry Night.

Nothing is wasted,
when viewed through the eyes of an artist.
Not even a single drop of coffee. And there
are no careless spills in the mind of a poet.

They all, in their own way, become paintings.
Not all masterpieces,
like Van Gogh's illustrious Starry Night.
But something meant to be, never the less.

The skies call out to all of us, though
few listen long enough
to allow their own interpretation to prevail.

The sky calls out to all of us for a reason.
But the reason is left to us to figure out.

Nothing is wasted, when seen through the
eyes of an artist – no careless spills ever
considered in the mind of a poet, no wasted

days, or utterly frivolous moments…we
create the
meaning of the life that we've been given.

And that, precisely, is the point!

4

Magnification

I could turn my telescope toward
the tree within – magnify a few of
the buds that will burst into life,
a mere 8-10 years from now. Or I

could remove all the lenses of probable
distortion, and simply see things
as they really are. Especially now,
in this early part of fall, just as the
world is beginning to allow the red glow

on the inside to shine out. While winter
waits patiently for leaves to drop from
the outstretched arms of well-rooted sentinels.

And I greet Tuesday, with a Sunday kind
of smile – the kind that many reserve for
only the most commercialized special occasions.

How absurd to wait for some preternatural,
well planned event,
marked on calendars,
primarily for the sake of retail sales.

How silly to sell yourself short,
and deprive yourself
of the gift of your own everyday.

Turn the goblet of great expectation upside down!

Let it fill in naturally, with what we
mistakenly refer to as nothing at all.

Turn the grand decanter upside down as well.
And the hourglass, spilling those sands of time
you have yet to claim as your own. Turn those too.

In any direction you now imagine might be better.
Turn it on its glassy side, and allow
the stardust, posing as sand, to be still for a time.

Turn it the way smiling toddlers turn
themselves, the instant they learn
how to. Turn the earth upside down,
then watch oaks, elms, and eager aspens

growing inward. And the narrow
tips of swaying cypress, pointing
down toward the heaven,
some elect to live in here on earth.

Turn it all upside down! The very
worse, best thing that could happen,
is that we
begin to see things as they really are.

Turn yourself upside down, and let
the small stuff discover the force of gravity.

Let the coins land where they may –
let the small things fall the way they
wish to – and let
the sunlight have its way with you.

Who among us, is not in need
of a true, warm, radiant embrace?

Sitting on a Wall of Stone

I remember leaning ladders against
a wall of stone when I was twelve –

climbing up the mud-stained rungs,
sitting high above the confusion

with a few of my boyhood friends.
The after-school gathering, the what-to-do

dilemma disappearing for the time
that sitting high seemed to be enough.

The natural dreams and wondering
what we might some day do, and

thus become – the world at our sneaker
covered feet, possibilities dangling from

those clouds above our heads.
Sitting high atop a stone wall,

feet hanging freely above the ground that felt
too confining for a young boys sensibility,

with the vividness of a ten plus two imagination…
too constricting for the longing

we feel when we are tender,
young and truly open to the world.

Falling Oranges and the Fruitful Absence of Boundaries

I brought no boundaries with me today
deliberately – only fresh imagery of
oranges falling from a wicker basket
onto an open blanket. Oranges and

innocence, spilling from my inner eye,
while I watch the many shinning
memories in the making. I didn't want
to come here today empty-handed –

the cracked tooth of temptation needing
to come out – splitting down the middle
like a wildflower growing straight through rock...
Not the common dandelions of doubt,

I'd rather not speak of those right now.
And I'm not referring to those overly
persuasive poppies of temporal euphoria.
Though they remain among the many

wild things, they aren't the ones I wish
right now to mention. Though they
share the soil with a thousand other
things, drunk now on a month of steady rain.

I didn't want to come here today empty handed,
even though the treasures I carry with
me are always counted. Better empty
handed than empty hearted, I suppose.

Better a cracked tooth than a shattered truth,
I suppose. Unless of course, the truth we
shatter, turns out to be a well constructed lie.
That then would be cause for celebration.

Would there be one less flower on the
earth tomorrow, if all the versions of the
many supposed holy books,
had been written in disappearing ink?

Would there be a less radiant sunset, if all
the printed pages, professing ultimate truth,
suddenly turned into unstained ivory,
allowing the emptiness to sing out as it's meant to.

String of Dreams

She told me about a string of dreams –
dreams of stallions swimming in a
powerful ocean, with waves reaching
heights of fifty feet. The night before

that, she dreamt of wounded lizards –
lizards long and green, with missing limbs –
hobbling amphibious creatures, with missing tails.

And there was one with a missing eye,
that wore a patch, and a head scarf, and drank dark
ale from a frothy metal mug.
And another stumbled by, that was totally blind.

And last night, she dreamt about a park in Chicago.
She went there to take in the sun,
while near-by buildings stood, casting
shadows on the grassy slopes and cement sidewalks.

She dreamt about a boy she met in high school –
the boy she later married…lived with, moved
with, grew with, raised two beautiful sons with.

That, she said, has been her dream come true.

The Transformation of Fine Bone-China

When a fine china saucer falls to the floor,
and its matching cup lands atop a marble
chessboard, shattering instantly upon impact,
into a larger number of pieces than we care
to count…we clean it up, and store the wholeness
of the moment in our memory, along with

the awareness that something came into being,
as a direct result of an apparently broken thing.
I suppose, if I had picked up all the shattered
pieces – collected each and every one of them
as carefully as I could, it might have been possible
to put it together again? Though it could never be the same.

It would never look, or feel, or function precisely
the same as did before that memorable moment of impact.
Or I could collect all the shattered pieces,
including the many dust-sized particles,

and turn them into something else…a fine china
mosaic, perhaps? Or three dimensional sculpture,
glued to a block of oak wood or mahogany.

Or I could combine all those fragments with other
materials – scrap metal, mixed with rock from
a nearby hillside, a single gold link from my mothers
favorite time-piece, some of the silver tips from the
empty pens, used to secure some of the meaningful
moments of a richly-lived life. And one precious jewel…

a diamond or emerald, fixed in the middle. And near
the bottom, I could include a small portion of a much
larger branch, cut from my Mimosa tree, and left on
the ground – by the men known to me only as tree trimmers.

Then I'll paint only the outer edges, and glue torn
and tattered photographs into all the corners, rip one full
page from my ever-ready Webster's, and paste it above the
jewel set in the center, showing how I place words

above diamonds or emeralds. I could pick a page
at random, with my eyes shut tightly, then imagine
it was chosen through divine selection. And above
the supremely selected page of perfect words, I could

include sheet music from one of Mozart's symphonies,
and a few drops of wax from a blood-red candle,
a finger full of dust from my living room window,

and a tiny fist full of fallen pine needles, turning gold
now as we speak. Plus six seeds from an unopened
grapefruit, waiting patiently in a porcelain bowl.

And maybe some of my own human hair?
Two gray, two brown, and one in the
midst of its own colorful transformation.

Then I'll add a little brown sugar, a dash of
cinnamon, and a hearty handful of whole,
complete, not-yet ground mustard seeds –

some of the spice of life, combined with an array of
other organic materials. Then stain the upper-most
edge with unstrained honey, giving
a sticky shine to my artful, everything kind of sculpture –

one that pleases the eye, triggers memories, fuels
the imagination, and attracts flies. Or it could turn out to be
a museum piece, with a living trail of ants. Or a thoughtfully

insightful, surreal kind of poem, inspired by the many fragments
of a shattered thing – bone china, colliding with
a marble chessboard, and becoming something else at the moment
    of impact.

Kneeling Down with
Later Day Saints & Poets

And in the later part of the day I
conduct my search – continuing
on near the outskirts of Sumatra.

Up the ever-moving mountain,
past the purgatoria and beyond
Dante's inferno. And when I reach

the summit of my late day quest,
I always feel compelled to kneel,
at least a little, out of respect for

my own wanting. And I never search
for or expect the final word. It's the
flutter that keeps me moving through

the day until it flows into tomorrow.
Mine is a rather raw, unpasteurized search.
Yes, there is the wanting and the

willing struggle, but different from
the flowers of Charles Baudelaire.
Different in nature from the evil he

tried to battle. He once recalled a
sunset, like a heart bleeding through
the sky from wounds of ruddy stain.

My search is rather different from
the one he did his best not to describe.
We all sense our own emptiness from

time to time – that sadness from the
world we leave behind. And who would
not wish to loose themselves in the

glow of an autumn sky? Or inside the
second morning of a radiant, one-time spring.
And so I continue my search through

the later part of the day – before nightfall,
and the Love and Barley of Basho –
before the hills ask me to write their

personal haiku, as the raven clears his
throat while staying hidden. And I continue
my search through the unwritten version

of Beowulf – me, the poet-warrior-prince
of my own province. And some see only the
shadows of golden haystacks – the opaque

wings of soaring crows, and the dark
spots in the sky that could be eagles.
As some embrace, and others condemn

the insights of truly auspicious artists…
and I continue in my search, late into the day, never the less.

Filling Up

And the world keeps filling up with
wonder – with the wind now racing

across oceans of potent invisibility.
The promise kept, the dancing light,

words and rituals, symbols and
misconceptions. The day, the dawn,

the darkness that always follows –
hidden in winter, bursting in spring,

the deep kiss of summer, the fiery
postulates of fall. The wind-filled awakening,

as the world keeps filling up with wonder.
Above, below, side by side, the terror

and the tenderness, the inscrutable
owl with its air of wisdom,

Carravaggio's rendition of the severed
head, blood-red at the neck, serpent

braids intertwined with our fear and
self-denial. The mystery, the majesty,

delight and disappointment, the crack
within the treasure we unearth.

The pantheon of greater possibility –
relics that were once our realizations.

And the world keeps filling up with
wonder . . . the morning always newly

made, the honey and rose-petals that
well surround the diatribe, hybrid dragons

painted on ancient papyrus, Persephone
still cloistered beneath the ground, with

the thoughts and understandings we need
now – the thoughts we need to help us

live above, now that Caspar is known
primarily as a friendly cartoon ghost.

Nothing holy, nothing sacred, nothing
connected to what we wish to honor most.

The memory, the meaning, the Magi,
now as vacant as the shadows of a fallen oak.

Looking Through

This is not a race for time, nor a seeking
to find the timeless. But rather something
delicately balanced between both;

a semi-surrealistic suspension between
the dream and what we refer to as the
waking world. Not the all-too-typical

transitional dangling between one fearful
possibility and another. No – not that . . .
not remotely. But rather, something close

to floating in the gentle pale-blue openness
of everything, like the perfect day repeated
for more than a century – always sensational,

though never quite the same. Much like the
first morning of forever, without the fiery explosion.

Of course, there are steady, small explosions
all the time; explosions of light and color,
explosions of sound from the center of deep silence,

explosions of thought, and the occasional fresh
idea that causes eruptions in the collective heart,
and great waves within the universal mind.

But mostly there is tranquil, empty space,
and blank pages left for us to fill – pages
that become our certificates of birth - blank

pages meant for us to fill, and thus become
our own autobiographical holy book or bible.
We look out and reflect upon the world that

we encounter . . .
we look up – into openness, emptiness,
endlessness and mystery. We look in,

and see essentially the same. We close our eyes,
fall asleep and discover the world again.
We look away and pretend that nothing

matters – the business, the overwhelm,
the intervals of rushing between the
seemingly endless tedium of waiting.

We look ahead and hope for something better.
We look back and weep for all those things we
have not done – for the dreams, that remained

dreams, that were forgotten. We look down,
with a heavy heart, and pray for something more.
We look through our confusion at the world we

filter through our pain. We look through terror
and murder and madness – through the lies we've
all been told - through politics, science, and

the dogmas of religion…we look, and see only
what we've been told that we should see.
We look and see precisely what we've been

conditioned to perceive. We look through
longing and see mostly what is missing –
the eye of intuition covered by the lid of false belief.

We look through greed and see only what
WE want, what WE think, what WE need.
We look for justice, and find hypocrisy.

We look through tenderness, and see abuse.
And still we continue to look and want and hope
and pray for a richer, brighter, better day.

And finally we look with love – through the eyes of love,

and see the perfect order of everything – we see
the glory, magnificence, and miracles,
through the ever astonished eyes of only love.

Taking Home Octavio

And I bent down to pick up Octavio –
kneeling before the alter of over a
hundred poets. I found Octavio standing
alone on the shelf – as alone as he

was in his life. I took him home, so that
we might listen alone-together – to the world,
in the twinkling, floating moment
of inconsistency – the jagged corners of deprivation,

the smooth stones embedded in cosmic sand,
and the bone-china, pale-blue, like the
faded shadows and frozen cracks of time,
the planetary saucer outlined in gold-lame,

fermentation, the moss of indecisiveness,
the potency of our own dreams,
fractal light breaking into everything – pyramids,
paradise, paradox, the prodigy of falling leaves

and dried emotions, visions shrunk down,
dehydrated, lying on the floor of our awareness,
near the moist lament of the many sunken ships,
where we find ghosts and those imaginary fornicating mermaids.

Ambrosia

Entrenched in the sense memory
of evening gowns and crystal
goblets – half-filled with ruby
liquid, half-empty, simultaneously,
with youthful drunkenness.

One might say: It was the night
that followed the full eclipse, the
majesty of those elaborate costumes,

and the sensuality of a naked
masquerade, wherein everyone
wore the lively spirit of another.

And the air was thick with laughter,
and the tension of summer love…
Amour – moist kisses dripping

from airy pedestals, promises meant
to be broken – softly spoken with
quivering voices, aided by undulating

tongues. One might say: It was a
sticky world, like caramel dreams,
melting through a poets utopia,
painted with panting heat clouds,

above moist air, aglow with fireflies.
One might say: It looked like a
liquid universe – lakes of morning
dew clinging luminously to everything,

making it impossible to sleep, while
covered in those passions that want
to wake us, like the rising tide that
meets the edges of a blanket near the

shore – soaking the threads of a late
night fantasy, that mixes with salty
liquid, and grows stronger with the
tenderness we dare to express in moonlight.

Celebration of Shadows

I did my best to collect the less-remembered
faces – the ones I saw standing alone on
empty streets, through the heat of a non-specific summer.

Those still in essentially the same spot,
on winter nights, that test the resolve of
poets, and claim the souls of would-be saints.

I did my best to hold them up – preserve a few of the wrinkles
of their largely obscure lives. I haven't lifted
them from the shadows, per se, but rather something else…

I carried many shadows into the fresh and luminous light.
Even the endarkened corridors,
are transformed by the softer rays of sunlight.

Even those pale-green faces, looking lost under
smoggy skies, adopt a richly different hue at daybreak.
And so I collect shadows,

that on the surface, appear to be other than my own.
And when I look into them, which I often do, I see the
differences, and I also see

how much they are the same – the degree to which
they closely resemble mine. One could say,
that daylight changes everything into shadow. Possibly?
Though if so, then it must be said: that shadow offers
energy to light, and darkness is a necessary consequence.

There are days, like the one unfolding now,
when I feel the sudden urge to wrap a fresh,
full loaf of French bread in my original baby blanket –
to cover the bread of life with my own innocence.

And to comfort the wide-eyed child that dwells within…
Nurture all that remains of my wild nature – keep it warm,
keep it vital, keep it fresh. There is so much
worth preserving, from where I sit. So much

worth remembering, from where I stand. So much well worth
savoring, from where I lie my head. Including the many shadows,
of course. As well as all those shades of blue,
providing the backdrop to my many voluptuous dreams.

And the gallons and gallons of cobalt blue,
that has permitted me to map the many, if not them all?
Those that a hundred years from now, will be the honored
charts, and cherished graphs of a solar-powered poets past.

A hundred years from now, as I hover over
a different balcony, that may resemble the
one I'm seeing now,
I know I'll be smiling about what I managed to lay down.

I know my ever-expanding heart will still be
dancing – soaring,
like those hawks that celebrate their ability to fly.
I'll be flying too! And celebrating my own ability –

hovering over the world I love, my light-filled spirit,
mingling buoyantly with some of the molecules of
my beautiful Mimosa tree.

A hundred years from now, I'll still be carrying
shadows into the light. And maybe, though I
can't say now for certain, I'll be wrapped once
more, in a brand new baby blanket.

Allowed to treasure the innocence over and over again.
Given the chance to look up again, into the shinning
eyes of another loving mother, and start it all over again.

What a natural, and sweet thing to consider – a profound
possibility for me to ponder. But this life now – the one
I'm fully living, is the richest, sweetest, most rewarding
one, that I can speak about now for certain. I will continue to
honor this life I've been given, and celebrate the shadow I cast now.

After 3:00 A.M.

Sometimes we say what can't be said,
while the common world is fast asleep,
as spiders spin their intricate
webs, beneath the cover of darkness.

Sometimes, after nightfall,
and the second wind begins to flutter,
while the empty bottles whisper
sonnets, through the shine of glassy green.

And I begin to remember the grace I
saw one summer, within the eyes of a beautiful young girl.
I thought at first, that it might have been a star.

Or a sacred, yet to be written trilogy, or possibly,
an untold epic poem. Or maybe only
a single line, from a simple, and timeless love song.

Then again, it could have been
the symphony of synchronistic heartbeats,
pounding away in the heat of mid-July,

following the balmy passion of an unexpected
thunderstorm – the lightening preceding
the crashing sounds,
offering us both a glimpse at our own eternal glow.

Where the Road Began

It was hot, and I had
nowhere else to go –
no place else I really
needed to be.

So I drove to
where the road began,
but never ended…
near those blossoms

of lavender springing
up near the trunks
of Poplar trees –
white bark peeling away,

revealing caramel-coated,
earthy rich sienna.
An empty bottle of
cobalt blue, littering

the ground, near those
rooted things I mentioned.
I sat in my car, behind
the rod-iron fence,

listening to blue
jays singing over
the traffic noise –
the sun creating a

sweat lodge inside
my dusty,
dark green Lexus.
And the lotus will

have to wait a while
longer – I'm busy now –
deeply involved, in what
some might see as nothing.

The Perpetual Absence of Metaphor

Raw almonds, Hawaiian honey, old friends,
new pens, the rounded doorway to a different
time, a blood-red candle, giving the light of itself
to an uncovered table, naked wood – exposed as

a poets passions, dreams, and visions, crows
squawking in the background of a rich and vibrant
moment, spools of yarn lying on the open road, next
to bobbins of silky thread – mounds of color beckoning
the spirit of one who knows they must weave their way

through the path that is their own, yellow markers,
crystal balls and crystal goblets, filled with the dizziness
of all those forgotten yesterdays, like a drunken moth falling
into an open flame, singeing its wings at the outer edges,

and surviving long enough to fly and fall again, before
becoming the graceful silhouette of something else,

above a field of barley, peppered with passionate red poppies,
swaying on a windless morning, with smiling yellow daisies,

listening to the archaic chants, and current whispers
of our time, that is the only time there truly is, though
we will continue to remember to forget – numb ourselves
with fear-based opiates, that help to justify the wide-spread

pastime of mindless obedience, while remaining prayerfully
oblivious to the sound, and voice, and call of our own soul,
though not without the deeply hidden desire to come to our
senses, and to build our personal monuments, before others

build our tomb – before we weep no more for our own
sense of rapture, and betrayal, as the quixotic colors fade
and fall, and the tiny nests of hummingbirds,
are exposed to winters song – there in the bare branches

of benign bewilderment, with frozen dew, giving an icy
shine to otherwise dull, gray bark, holding the verdant
memory of once thirsty leaves, drinking rain and radiant

sunlight, and those daydreams that woke us up in a
whole new way – evoking barren poems, that began
to flower, and speak out loud, offering literal fruit,
bitter and sweet, salty and bland, poignant and persistent,

like timelessness, and the mind of a truly loved child – loved,
fed, nurtured, and needed, allowing them to be naturally playful
and fearless – the opposite of nearly all our conditioning,

that denies the truth, and obfuscates much of the of
human history, steeped in ritual, tradition, superstition,
and hunger…for everything our abundant world has
to offer; meat and bread, fruit and wine, nuts and dates,

the patient fermentation of our deep, organic thoughts,
dreams, visions, and medieval mystery, that facilitates
the resurrection of our true self, before the turmeric, and
salt of life is scattered through the force of faulty winds,

brought about by men that cling to only crass imagination,
wishing to extinguish any and every artful thought, that
could bring about the beauty of truthful expression, and

permit us to bare witness to the fruits of our own sacred,
splendid, spectacular, seminal harvest.

Listening to Nightfall

Listen with me now, as if
you're remembering ecstasy.
Take me in like those clouds

we see at sunset, with an
astonished smile
we simply can't control.

I see the hilltops with their
early twilight shadow –
nothing speculative, the utter
absence of anything random –

the perfect plan, with a fresh
slice of luminous blue, and the great
fortune of bare branches, winters

winters wooden arms, evoked by
frigid wind, and hidden tunnels
beneath the halloed ground.

I call this splendor,
and the ravens all agree.
Even the argumentative

albatross nods his head
in agreement, and I nod
back through green and

white umbrellas.
I am a fortunate man –
husband, father, son.

I am a graceful friend –
a human pendulum proclaiming
my own balance, as the city

shouts at itself, and condemns
some less fortunate souls.

Then I listen to seagulls soaring
above my head, and remember
summer's dandelions – the
quixotic yellow dance, before

the ivory transformation –
the gusting winds and gentle
breezes that carry their seeds

to faraway places, while children
sleep tucked beneath the covers
of their colorful dreams that

want to be remembered –
fruitful visions that beckon
recognition, and the vigor
of open-eyed innocence.

The initiation of the still
uncluttered mind,
before the judgement and
frozen emotion…

before the consequence of
our own hunger – the tender,
fleshy satisfaction we all crave.

The wonder we find
everywhere, especially
at twilight,
standing alone looking
at perpendicular hilltops,

with their haunting silence
and savage softness, that
make children of all ages

want to fly to them, and swear
their allegiance to the elegance
of nature's mysterious order.

No Way Back

I needed to get out today, after being
sequestered for nearly a decade inside
that granite mountain, searching for
the ever-elusive diamond mine.

Now the world is asking me for
everything, and I wish only to comply.

And it doesn't matter where I left
off yesterday, or where I imagine
or pretend to begin today…

Maybe I'll move to New Mexico
and let my beard grow. Allow my
gray-brown whiskers to soften my

fleshy marble chin, and dance with
some of the other artists of my day.

Maybe I'll climb to the top of a sacred
mesa – watch a sunset through the
eyes of a brand-new man and permit
my thoughts to fall like quiet rain.

Then I'll dry my emotions with the open
end of a one-time only rainbow – catch
salmon in a bubbling brook,
and cook my lucid dreams a little longer.

Maybe I'll stain an empty canvas with
unstrained honey, ancient sand and half
a glass of Elderberry Wine, then carve
a bow from a willing branch – a bendable

Cypress or pliable Oak…mold my arrows
from hardened stardust and fashion tips
from skipping stones. Maybe I'll shoot
straight this time…? Hit my target dead center,

then dance home again, stopping along
the way to see and smell and savor
all the roses, daisies, tulips, and erupting wildflowers.

And if all the crumbs I scattered along
the way, have been feasted upon by
tiny birds that never learned,
but always knew exactly how to pray…

I won't feel the least bit lost, knowing all the
while, that there never was a way of getting back.

Sacrifice in Full Bloom

Single rose standing in
the rain, babies breath

blowing around your
severed stem, crystal

walls of water keeping
you alive a little longer,

signature scent still
hovering above your

velvety blood-red dome.
Standing so alone now

atop my deep green
patio table – a single

flower, solitary rose,
cut for the sake of a

saint by the name of
Valentine…

for the sake of love,
for the sake of tenderness,

the sake of softness,
the sake of grace…

your stem severed, along with
the dream that our love might bloom.

The Opening of O'Keeffe's Flowers

How many times can I expect O'Keeffe's
flowers to fully open up to me? Can I keep
asking her over-sized ivory roses to continue
blooming, even though they were painted in
the 1940's? And what about her black abstractions,

or her blood-red magnolias, or those sensuous hills,
with their moist flowing folds, reminding us of mountainous
vaginas. What is it about her art that draws
me in and draws me out? I wouldn't necessarily want
to get lost forever in those lively folds,
that blend so smoothly and naturally into the landscape.

Or become a cave dweller – building my fires
on the inside of an earthy womb, beyond
the soft pink entryway to temporal paradise.

Although there have been times – periods of my life,
in which I thought I wanted nothing more than to live
and die there – days and nights wherein I thought I did.

Now I give fire to colorful candles, every morning after
leaping out of bed. I build my fires on the outside, then I go in.
And that's precisely what keeps bringing me back to O'Keeffe.
Back to her over-sized roses and cloud-like magnolias.

Back to her earthy hills, with their sensuous folds.
And who else has painted a portion of the Brooklyn Bridge,
appearing as stained glass windows within a holy city cathedral?

And now I'm drinking coffee from fine bone
China – black and white, with 18k gold leaf trim,
Tuscan fine English Bone China to be precise.
The league of nations in an artful cup and saucer.

I'm tempted now to say something about Tuscany…
at least mention the serene grandeur of those
luminous hills that surround the tree-lined countryside.

Then move on to China's Great Wall, then straight to
England to take in a panoramic view of Cornwall,
at the southernmost point, close to the Atlantic.

But I feel the need to get back to O'Keeffe –
     back to her ever-opening
flowers and giant vaginas. Back to the real world cathedral,
with its widely open unstained windows we find everywhere.

Maybe getting lost again in soft pink folds would
do me a world of good? Or do me in, dependent upon
the particular folds I permit myself to get lost in?
It might be safer to seek out some of the well built
cathedrals of the world – take snapshots of the exquisite

stained glass windows, and marvel at the captivating
architectural designs. It's always safer to admire the
ornate structure made from wood and brick and glass
and stone, than it is to be irresistibly moved by the
artful structure of a sensuously inviting human being.

Regardless of how large and elaborate a building might be,
we can always leave it without getting our heart broken.
Walking in and out of ancient or modern marvels, is always

easier than walking in and out of the life of someone we once loved.
How many times can I expect O'Keeffe's flowers
to fully open up to me? I think I know now…as often as I open
    up to them!

Melding With Moonlight

You told me; this cannot be utopia …
the fabric is as weightless as evaporating sea mist.
We can't let all our hopes and dreams
rest upon things that may never learn to fly!

Come dance with me, the world
will be here when we get back …
though it will never be the same.

Climb with me to my rooftop – lie
with me in the open sun, and permit
this warm laconic winter to have its way with us.

Listen with me to the stampede of our hearts –
the pounding hoofs of wonder and astonishment –

rising with our passion, like a ladder
to the stars – love, the lifeline to our
drowning dreams, your radiant smile
and tender touch is the only food I need.

I cannot take back that which I've
given freely … It is yours!
And yours, I know now, is mine.

Now we melt like moonlight through
the tender open end of our oblivion.

What More

And what more can be done, once
the tender departure from sorrow
is complete, and the eyes of the world

continue to open and close throughout
the days and nights of every shifting
decade – when we get to a grand beginning,

and mistake it for a moment of the
end, and the wind-swept whispers
become a choir of contented voices

singing together to guide the deaf
ones home – and we invent our own
sense of time that allows us to correct the days

we know we could have lived better,
 had we but listened in alignment with
our soulful intuition, instead of sacrificing

our vital organs for a single-endless stream
of indiscretions, while removing the screen
that prevents the dust from forming

on the surface of that which only light
should touch, leaving the sonnets of
indecisiveness to those with the need

to stay behind – those that pamper themselves
with portfolios of false pride, permitting

the weeds of self-destruction to grow
wild, until they overwhelm the roses.

Awakened by the Glow of New Grapes

I saw the new grapes glistening,
even before I made my leap from bed.
They woke me up this morning –
those shinny purplish red orbs of

sweet opportunity. Morning dew
covering the steadily shifting shades
of lively crimson – a delightful
array of color to be reawakened with.

New grapes, dangling from that inner vine,
begging to be picked – asking to
be squeezed – dying to be savored.
Colorful grapes, on a grand horizon, and
a smooth earthy stone pointing towards them.

And an ivory pumpkin, with a firm,
jagged stem, reaching from the center of itself –
an almost colorless gourd, resting
on the left side – a multi-colored container of
liquid passion waiting on the right.

Last night I ventured out alone to capture
the watercolors… I wanted to take them
in, the way we sip rare wine – those
exquisite vintages we dare not waste a drop of.

The ones we drink in with our deep and
precious secrets, as we permit our quiet
laughter to soar to boundless heights,

where it can reach out and touch a multitude
of exploding stars. And we feel compelled to
go there with it. I wanted to see the world directly,

in all its artful glory, fully prepared to weep,
if I feel moved to. I went out to capture the
watercolors, and allow them to fully capture me.

And I did precisely that – without any
second guessing, or utterly unnecessary restraint.

It's so amazing to see rocks come to life on
paper, or to watch them start to roll across
a tightly stretched, presumably once-white canvas.

Or to be able to pick up the inspired scent
of wild roses,
even though they lack the third dimension.

Then witness a single petal of pale lavender,
falling from the top of a tall, proud iris –
falling beyond the boundaries of textured paper –
bleached white, and thirsting for new pigment.

Then stepping into the painted page to pick up
the quixotic petal that fell an instant ago, and
place it back upon the stem I watched it fall from.

I went out alone last night, to capture some of the
scents and shades and sounds of the living world.
I went out to take in the watercolors,
and fill the well that permits me to keep giving.

Last night I was drawn into the dark
and muted realms; into shadow, mystery,
and stark reflection. I watched a light

brown deer, drinking from the mouth of
its own image –
quenching its thirst in the shallows of black water.

And I saw bedouins wearing white and rich royal blue.
And a gondola floated under an old Venice bridge.
And I glanced briefly at a handful
of harsh abstracts, that I felt no real urge to understand.

I loved looking at the rain clouds – gray and
white, with measured streaks of polymorphous yellow.

And the rites of spring commanded
my attention – capricious as it
always is; eager,
energetic, and wild as it's truly meant to be.

Coming Back to the Watercolors

I knew I'd come back to the watercolors,
even though I swam
inside them throughout most of yesterday.
They filled in my day – evoking thoughts,
and adding color to my never-dry palette of emotion.

I had a feeling I'd return to them again today –
we always want more of what really feeds us.
I love those tender shades – the ones that

flood forth for little more that a graceful hour,
in order to make their grand
announcement of the good that's here right now!
And I love the reds that want
to wake us and warn us all to really pay attention.

Those foreboding flowers that wilt before our
barely open eyes, urging us to make our contribution
to the world before we wilt with them.
And the endless greens that offer us a new sense
of fertility, within the verdant splendor of what we're meant to be.

And I would never neglect the grandeur of those
shades of yellow-gold, or the
rapture of pure ivory, or the glory of moist quixotic pink.
And wherever I go, I keep coming back
to the many lively shades of crimson – like those
shinny grapes, still on the vine, glowing in afternoon sunlight.

Or at the end of the day, as they change
their color, against the background of fiery burnt-orange.
Changing into their evening attire, preparing for
the birth of a billion new stars, while
reacquainting themselves with some of the really old ones.

I knew I'd come back to them today –
to the new shades of the old forever colors.
I knew I'd return to the watercolors,
and I knew I would for all the right reasons.

Not the way that ravens return to carrion –
to make a meal of putrefying flesh.
Though not entirely different from it either.

I keep coming back to the watercolors,
because my soul keeps wanting to be fed.

I come back to feast again upon fresh color – the fresh,
lively, vibrantly promising palette of truly new color.
I keep coming back because I want to see what's new.
Color makes the whole world bright and new –
everything, the eyes we look through, in particular.

And when we see the world through new eyes,
we remake it, by virtue of the vision we allow.
And as we make our world, we make ourselves.

Then we're free to weep, because we finally know true beauty.
Then we can laugh, because the madness can't possess us.
Then we can speak from the heart of what we know for ourselves.
And come back to the watercolors, because we choose to.

We return again and again for all the right reasons…
to feast upon those things that feed us directly; the beauty,
color, love and passion that nurtures
us repeatedly, and frees us from the bondage of confusion.

And from the fear of never knowing quite enough.
And from the paralysis of pretending we already know it all!
I had a feeling I'd come back to all those colors today.

Because the truth is, we can never get enough…
at least not enough to say we've now had enough.
Sometimes all we really need, is a fresh coat of paint,
on an old, dull, lackluster, dust-covered door.

Clean it first – dust it off, wash it down from top to bottom.
Then give it a fresh new color – a new coat of paint.
Then open it, and what you find on the other side,
may surprise you, for the first time in too many years.

Habitat for Troubled Hearts

We talk about natural
habitat – the untamed

places, those wild,
rhythmical regions,

where Saskatoon and
fragrant Sagebrush

grow side by side, while
bees make thick amber honey.

There, in the thicket
of dogwood, clusters

of Bearberry, and a Bur Oak
growing in-between them.

A place where people
lose their way, cutting

paths through the center

of paradise, in order
to quickly get beyond it.

Where is the natural
habitat of the wild

human heart?
Atop the mesa, or

untamed metropolis?
Atop those mountain

peaks covered in
untouched snow?

Or in the valleys of
frightened consistency,

from where leaps are
rarely ever made.

Shadow Walk

My shadow led the way along
the dirt path – that earthy

byway lined with tiny rocks,
and sizeable stones.

Upward in the noonday sun…
Follow me, my shadow said,

stay with me,
and try to keep up.

First the steep ascent – the winding
path, around the

bend and up again.
Blue birds landing in the cover

of sagebrush and bramble bush,
the sounds of bees ,

daylight filtered through
scattered clouds –

climbing, climbing – keep up,
my shadow says.

Follow me, I know the way...
the ascending spiral towards

the sun.
Keep up, we're heading

down now.
Descent, ascent, it's all the same,

my shadow says – light above,
light below, essentially there

is no difference – the source of
up and down is quite the same.

Stay with me, I know the way,
I've led you this far,

don't abandon me now.
Look up! The sky holds

our visions, hopes,
dreams and possibilities.

It's much easier
to catch the world

when our eyes are open.

Really Wanting it All

For a moment I thought I just might want it
all today? All the cities, all the towns,
as well as all the widely open territory.
Every exotic country I've yet to visit – every landscape,

in every dream I've ever had, including all the oceans
I'd need to cross. Every strange, hideously
beautiful life-form that has ever lived within them.
Every phosphorescent fish that swims

beneath the surface. Every blue-gray
dolphin sailing above the waves.
Every killer whale. Each and every
octopus, giant squid, and tiny sea-horse

floating in watery suspended animation.
And all the islands, surrounded by all those
oceans that I have not mentioned
yet by name. I want them all! Or thought I

might, a moment ago. And I want
the largest fine art collection ever
imagined…all the Picassos,
including his over-sized sculptures, early sketches,

as well as those thirty foot canvases,
he painted in his nineties – near the
end, as he turned into a child again.
And I want all that's left of Dalis' burnt giraffes.

And all the paintings – framed, unframed,
and undecided. And all the unfinished
canvases as well – all the projects that
his genius didn't permit him to complete.

I want every crucifix he loathed and loved
simultaneously. I want every bloody cross,
that any tainted saint has ever hung from.
And the bloodless ones as well.

And those that were ignited by the fear we
allowed to harden into hatred. I want all
the burnt and bloodied crosses
that ever stood in for our actual humanity.

I want them all – here and now, in one well lit,
convenient central location. And I want to
rescue all the bones of slaves that can't find
peace at the bottom of the Atlantic ocean.

I want to carry them to the surface and
reassemble them, and when they've all
been reassembled, I want to gather them
all together, ask them to form an enormous

circle, that I will enter, sit in the middle of,
and simply listen. I will listen, weep, and
allow them to offer me counsel. And I will
answer any question any drown, forgotten

slave might wish to ask of me. And if I
have no honest answer, I will look into
their missing eyes, and tell them I don't know.
I want all the art…every dance

that's ever been done, book written, photograph
taken, and story ever told. And music…
I want every bit of it! Every note, every rhythm,
beat, melody and harmonious sound.

Every folk song that ever started as a prayer
or poem or longed for possibility. Every Bach
sonata, Beethoven symphony, and every
nocturne of Rochmaninoff, Chopin, and Bizet.

And I want all the drama – all the laughter, all
the pain, and all the tears. And I want all the
terror too – all we can possibly muster, all at once.
I want the deepest sadness, and the highest bliss.

I want all the color, every star, and every rainbow.
And all the sunsets ever seen by human eyes –
all the thoughts, emotions, hopes and dreams
evoked by letting in the brightest light imaginable.

I want the wings of every raven, hawk, and
eagle that ever soared through any open sky.
And I want every humming bird
and hovering butterfly as well, and all the

blossoms, buds and flowers that they flock to;
all the roses, all the tulips, all the poppies and
daisies dancing and swaying in every open field.

And for a moment I thought I just might

want it all today…then I realized…I have it.

Written in Rain

The sandbox has been turned
into a pond. Or a tiny lake
of light brown rippling water.

A sudden noise caused all the
crows to fly away, as I swim

back through my most recent
day – through endless rain,

moist memories, and haunting
whispers from a wet and empty balcony...

my world – my kingdom for one
kiss, or well written sonnet to

blend with the new carpet, laid
wall to wall, and the sweet scent

and color of friendship, with its
passion on every side. I make

little time these days , for would-be
saints, or silent wood-nymphs
that refuse to sing their heart song,

or echo what all the well-rooted
eager trees are willing to whisper.

Ecstatic Sculpture

The gifts are everywhere we dare to look.
I see them in a single drop of wax – the
dripping fortunes of our time.
I see it now, within the deep burgundy branches

of winter plum trees – dropping leaves
that match the color of rare French wine.
I see them in the things
I know, as well as in the strange and unfamiliar.

To a large degree, we see what we're willing
to see – what we're willing to open up to,
and take in. Vision is in the heart and mind,
as much as it is in the eyes which we look out from.

I'm seated inside now, looking out at my perfectly
round patio table. I think I may move out there very soon?

Pick myself up, grab my simple belongings,
and reposition myself at my outdoor patio table.

The air is so artfully cool, alive, and compelling.
I'm standing now, preparing to make my move
in to the outside world. I'm outside now – swirls

of impassioned ivory, paint the lower portion of
this blue overhead eternity. Shifting swirls of ivory,

beginning to look like mounds of radiant clay. . .
mounds of radiant clay, waiting to be sculpted.

If I could reach them from where I'm sitting,
I would attempt to mold
this ethereal clay, into a
lively human torso, twisted into an artful

shape of ecstasy. I would shape it on all three
sides, then fill it in with poetry and laughter,
and allow the fertile wind to have its way with it.

Then, while still seated at my perfectly
round patio table, I would raise my eyes
up, and say to myself; look what we made now!

We made a beautiful human torso, from the
likes of ethereal clay – something to cherish
deeply, before it disappears, or floats away.

Before moving swirls become a solid sheet
of white – a pallor of ordinary ivory, like
bleached papyrus waiting to be written on.

A now pale promise, asking to be colored in
with an array of phrases, from the silver-tipped
pen of a pantheistic poet, able to offer genuine
praise for the sacred and natural world.

Before the sheet of white is washed away
by ancient wind – by the breath of poets,
friends, and lovers,
from those realms that we imagined were long past.

They hover over us again, settle down
around us,
look us in the eye, and give their smile.

And now we must decide for ourselves,
whether or not we're willing to let them in?

Can we trust them this time? Can we trust ourselves?

Will we dance this time, when the grace
of our own movement is so desperately needed?
Will we sing out when the silence beckons,
and hush the fears that threaten to hold us back?

And will we be willing, this time, to shape
those clouds above our head – mold the shinny
ethereal clay into an artful shape of ecstasy.

Then look in, and smile deeply at what we've done.

Unclaimed Grace

Where is the grace within
the words we never utter –
the litany
of sounds we never make?

Rarely do we see grace
within the bumps we
get from falling down.

Or within the bruising of our
broader sensibilities,
when the outcome of
our attempts fall short of what
we so passionately envisioned.

Where is the grace within the polar
opposites of possibility – within the
full and sacred scope of our desire?

With all our feckless attempts
to leave behind a shining and
spotless lineage…wait a minute!

Then wait again.

Where is the grace in our refusal
to kiss and embrace
the life that we've been given,

while we stumble over our daily bread,
and slide across the blood of all our ancestors.

Om-mission

I heard something about the sin of
omission, though I can't remember
who I heard it from? Or where I
was, at the moment my omission
was re-birthed? Or why? It had

something to do with the color gold,
like the flowing hair of a glowing
Goddess, peering into the lavender
center of a water lily, while seated
silently at the edge of a pristine pond.

Then again, it may well have been a
wheat field – bending to the wind on
a radiant September morning, offering
a vainglorious reminder. It may have been.

Though I can't yet say for certain, unlike
the streaks of burgundy, spilling before me
from the branches of late summer plum trees,
beneath the china-blue dome of a sun-drenched sky.

Or the torment of daisies, under the flashing
feet of more than a thousand ecstatic dancers,
or a single dandelion, in the hand of an open-eyed child.

What more can we do, but pluck the pleasures from
the place we are right now? Then decide for ourselves,
which ones we're willing to admit to? And which will
remain among the sins, within the glory of our omission?

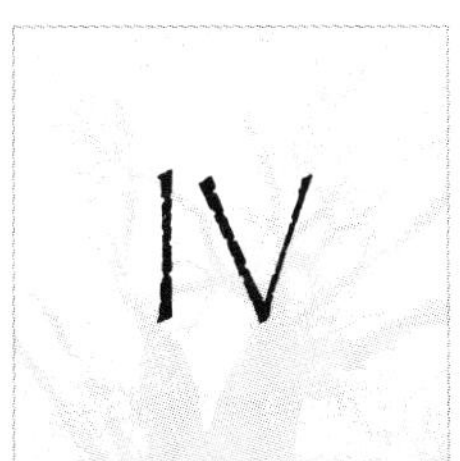

Selected Solitudes

There's such a wide variety of solitudes –
the empty ones, as well those so full
the great canyons of the world can hardly
hold them. I remember my solitary train

rides, attempting to capture the entire
world at every turn – trying to take it
all in and keep it for more than a day.
Wanting to capture as many faces as

humanly possible, including the ones
I raced by while the train wheels screeched
passed streets and buildings at sixty miles

per hour… And what is speed, but a cousin
to the illusion of time. I learned to slow
them both, on some of my morning train rides.

There is such a wide variety of solitudes…
I remember some of the dry ones, like ancient
pottery, complete with cracks that allude
to the tested mark of fate and self-made character.

And I remember some of the moist ones too,
and a few of the wet ones, dripping with wine,
and tasting of laughter. I've known a wide
array of soft and tender solitudes, as well

as the firm ones, and some of the razor-sharp ones,
that cut me wide open, while I danced through
the pageantry of my own perception. And I've
known the ones that were aged, spiced, sautéed,

simmered, and served on elegant platters,
and though I thought I mostly enjoyed them
in the moment, in retrospect, I can say for certain,
that I favored the ones picked fresh, and offered raw.

I've seen the one sided solitudes and I've
explored the multidimensional. I could
probably name them all, though they
can't be numbered. Those that are stationary,

and those on the move. The noisy ones and
those I savored in the depths of my own
silence – the serene solitudes and those

that demanded chaos. I've been inside
the smooth, round, really centered ones.
And I've ventured into a few of the rough,

rectangular, entangled ones, with nothing
but jagged edges. But most of the time I
select the ones that I'm not afraid to let cut me open.

Monday's Child

I brought it all today; whole grain bread,
amber honey, protein powder – undenatured,
micro-filtered peptides of greater possibility…

easy to mix, and rather pleasant tasting.
And that's not all! Not nearly all.

I'm holding the stone of life in my left
hand, and the bridge over untroubled
waters is still standing.

And an unwrapped fortune cookie,
looking like the carefree crescent moon,

with many windows – rounded windows,
with open, eager faces peering through.

The reflections of night and day, with
nine muses dancing nearly naked around

a rocket ship, far and away from the time-line
we created from our illusion of thin air.

And the music I first heard live, begins
to trickle out through three foot speakers,
that remind me to remember–sounds.

that lift me to the level of laughing and
weeping, and ease
the angst that often accompanies our
deep, abiding sense of really wanting.

The listening that reminds us to really listen.
I brought it all today; protein, honey, and the
bread of life…sacred stones, the scent of glory,

the texture of friendship,
and all those tastes I wouldn't allow myself to miss.

I carried it all to my fine wood table,
by candle-light, below the edifice of castle walls,

and those medieval arches that lead us to the
garden, within the
courtyard of our greatly needed Renaissance.

Those guardedly open spaces, intended to
appease the endless need for artful beauty,

love, comfort, warmth
and a respectful understanding of our own.

The need of cities with cobblestone streets, that
inspire, and instruct us to slow down. We need

to feel what we find beneath our feet – dirt, sand,
cement, or ancient cobblestone…all are good,
in their own way. They all provide us with something

we can walk upon – something we can step
across, in our own time. Streets, roads, bridges,
byways – pathways to the many gateways,

and beyond – all the way to those sacred tunnels,
that take us to the heart of who we are.

All the way through to the unknown regions, that
beckon us, and beg us to provide them with a name.

Those open roads that call us out, those pristine
realms that reel us in,
and encourage us to become our own true witness.

To break open the fortune cookie of our own
making,
and really savor it, for the first and only time…

Then to place our own good fortune in
the center of what we know is truly good.

Deeper Than My Own Delight

It seems necessary, to me, that I go deep today…
deeper than the typical delights I dance with every day.
Deeper than Dali's rendition of Narcissus kneeling
near the shinny edge of a reflecting pool – even
deeper than Don Quixote's desire for only true action.

I need to go there today, of my own volition – past the
center of my one time struggle. Deeper than last year,
last month, or even yesterday – as all the
still clinging leaves began expressing their hidden shades.

Really deep – beyond those blood-red borders
that surround the blue-gray folds that line the
entryway to that dark, though sometimes tempting abyss.
Deeper than that – beyond those frozen moments of time,

where lightning struck the purple perimeter of someone
else's thoughts, beliefs, and imaginings of heaven.
Really deep! Past the home of Persephone's abductor –
deeper than the winter home of Demeter's youngest daughter.

Deeper than all my dreams of Africa—more to the
core than my remaining Asian fantasies. Even deeper

than all my Mediterranean memories. I need to dig
today – all the way to the bottom of
Pandora's box, where hope lies waiting to be claimed.

And when I get to it, I plan to lift it from its
muddy bottom, and carry it back to the surface.
Though something must be given in exchange –
something to leave in the spot where hope was stored…
something to place within the otherwise murky emptiness.

And I know just what it will be. I'll replace the hope I take,
with some of the sorrows that were let loose long ago –
the sorrows of humanity,
that once rested on the bottom where hope now lies.

I'll carry some of those sorrows with me,
and give them in exchange for the hope that's needed now.

After all, both grew together long ago – incubating
at the bottom of Pandora's box. Then the box was
opened, a little too quickly I presume,
with the kind of carelessness that sometimes overwhelms

our healthy curiosity. It was merely a matter of
eagerness overshadowing our skill and human
experience, allowing the many sorrows to escape,
while leaving hope stuck on the bottom, tangled in eagerness.

And so today I will make a careful and conscious
exchange – sorrow in exchange for the hope that we need now.
And once the exchange has been made – hope secured,
and sorrow left on the bottom, then I'll carry hope to the surface
     and set it free!

Then I'll be free to continue my journey downward…
it's necessary, for me, that I go deep today.
Deeper than the sorrows of a broken heart,
that once wounded me, and healed me simultaneously.

And some wounds are intended not to heal – the ones
that always seem to carry their own opening – the ones
that stay fresh and raw and vital throughout our lifetime.
We may guard them – cover and protect them,
still they remain the wounds we literally learn to live with.

Some are made from sorrow mixed with hope, which turns
to love, that fuels the process of our own true transformation.

And when daylight calls me back, I won't resist…
I went deep today…willingly, into the subterranean
darkness rather eagerly, and I will rise again in the same way.

I love daylight, though I no longer fear the darkness.
And when I return to the surface , I'll stop to visit Apollo…
listen to topside music, and share my recent poetry, in exchange
        for his.

The Goddess of my own Time

Time hangs gracefully over the edges
of my artful table – one comfortable
corner of history, dangling upon the

surface of forever, while a lovely Goddess
rests in a wooden bowl, with glowing skin,
and flowing hair, draped across the organic
fabric of her ivory gown. She waits for me…
inside a wooden bowl, near a pristine pond.

Lost within the serene beauty of a water lily.
Lost in the lavender center of her awareness.
Lost inside the solitude that permits her to see herself.
Lost within the dream she needs to share.

Her heart sinks, then soars. Her mind wanders.
She laughs quietly, then wipes one tear from her radiant cheek.
She sings to herself, and the forest that surrounds her
    echoes back.

The leaves adore her. They change color in her presence.
They love her artful spirit of aliveness.
They turn red and yellow to impress her.

They turn orange to match the highlights in her hair.
They turn brown, and fall all around her perfect feet.

She is pure emotion. She is light and love.
She is everything and nothing all at once.
She is a figment of my own imagination –
the energy that adds color to the creation of my world.

She is as real as I am willing to allow –
as vibrant as the sunrise, if I need her to be.
As articulate as the wind, carrying
information rooted to my deepest, true desire.

She waits for me and me alone, because I am the only poet alive
that knows how to wake her. She waits for me,
because together we hold the power to wake each other.

She is pure emotion – a vital part of my true life force.
She is the current within the flow of my own thought –
my colorful mistress, my brilliant flame, my artful temptress,

my great glowing Goddess of mid-life.
She is the reason I remember – the ache
in my heart that won't permit me to forget.

She is the reason I woke up today.
She is the promise I made to myself – and kept!
She is the urge to continue telling my story truthfully.

She waits for me and me alone, because I am
the only poet alive that knows where to find
her – the only man who knows how real she is.

She skins her knee on ancient stone,
and only her luminosity bleeds out…

Days of Questionable Wonder

There are days, like this one, that make
oblivion sound better than it did yesterday.

Days when looking at black and white
photographs of someone else's summer
camp, is consoling, in some strange, slightly
somber way.

Days that have nothing to do with the
weather per se – moods not completely
void of sunshine, though they wouldn't
all that easily be mistaken for bliss.

Afternoons, while sitting at the end of a
park bench, near the unwashed feet of a
sleeping monk, well-disguised, in the
tattered clothes of a homeless alcoholic,
and you feel shaken to the core of your own humanity.

On those hot and sunny afternoons, when you
secretly wish for rain – those mid-day hours,
you sit pining away for the following morning,
while resurrecting
memories of that summer you first fell in love.

There are days, like this one, when falling
off the earth somehow seems possible,
even though we know the earth is round.

Days you can't help wondering
whether life was any easier,
back when everyone
knew for certain the earth was flat?

On those late afternoons when you keep
seeing faces in all those withering flowers,
and you know the wind that keeps
kissing the back of your head is your grandfather.

Dreaded Intention Turned into Delight

Somehow it all made sense back then…
in the middle of that winter, when I
devirginized half the girls on my block,
and the olives fell like peaches from inside
a bloody anvil.

And I melded myself from their willingness,
and built myself from the iron of my own resistance.

The thing is, I didn't try, it all just happened, naturally,
the way Peter Pan came looking for my mother,
and found fireflies. And it wasn't our cruelty that

made us tear off their glowing bellies to wear as rings,
but our hunger, and a drop or two of unplanned madness
that we began to sacrifice on the alter of a magazine.

And I fell in love with Joni Mitchell repeatedly,
when I was an eager envelope to be sent first class
into the jungles of East Africa, near Schweitzer's
makeshift hospital, on the outskirts of my doctor's orders.

But that was a long time ago, and I've become grass
before the early part of spring, though not without a
morsel of regret, and a pinch of semi-sweet chocolate,

that she savored with her eyes shut tightly, telling me;
it tasted just like 40,000 angels fornicating on her tongue.

Though it's still pretty cold in Sweden in mid-winter,
especially off the wall of mud, where that spider
laid it's eggs and asked for mercy. But that really

doesn't matter anymore. What matters is the dust
on the wings of butterflies, and the way mustard seeds

float on stagnant waters, before fertility, and the birth
of dead ideas, that move us backward, away from
the middle, then tempt us to accept it as an end.

Then I asked you to stop weeping for the long lost
sheep and scattered dreams, and simply dance with
me, the way you did in Brussels,

and on the Portuguese coast, where we wore tablecloths
as rain-gear over our sweaty nakedness,
then watched the storm upon my promise to be good.

And you...you were beautiful, and just as willing as
the rainbow that marked the death of innocence, and we
slept until the wine was ready, then sang that
wheat field below the ground...do you remember?

Spicy Hunger in the Later Afternoon

What then would I feast on if all my
words dried up and left me empty?

All the unpicked inner grapes left to
whither on their dreamy, wild vine and
the To Kill a Mockingbird tree fell over.

What if I licked my fingers clean of
all the salt left from the tempest I
tasted yesterday, the shells cracking open

on their own, though void of protein,
and I said no to the moving mountain,
because it only carried me closer to my own emptiness.

Then while fixing my well-pressed collar,
I discovered chocolate, then heard the
laughter from the other side, beyond
the steam of some of the more fragrant possibilities.

And I wondered where you were this
afternoon, as I remembered
your lilac skin and luminous smile.

If I saw you now, I'd want to lift you
up and carry you into my balmy,
well-lit underworld – for glory, tea,
and tidbits of the many things we fancy.

And when we felt full enough, we could
dance again, then fall naked on the floor
of my well-imagined castle, while sharing the ultra-violet

colors of our dreams, forgetting the sound
and meaning of fortune birthed from steady,
willful, colorful anxiety.

And we wouldn't need the myths found
in modern magazines to remind us who we are.

Or to tell us where we already know that we belong.

Then I could kiss the tops and bottoms of your
toes, after removing your shinny silver
sandals, and tell you again how beautiful you are.

Early Morning Answer

I sit here in my relative silence, listening
to some of the ancient expressions, carried
into my present on currents of mid-October wind.

And I can't help but wonder what these winds want?
What do these pleasant gusts, in their
sweeping glory, and warm grace, have to say?

And who is qualified to interpret their moving,
airy language, if not a poet fully powered by the sun!
How many prayers for peace, taken by wind,

and widely circulated, are at this instant, rustling
through the branches at the edge of my balcony?
I can only wonder, as I peer into the steady flame,

atop my dripping, teal blue candle, and ask,
what I want from myself today? It's best to
ask yourself such questions, especially when

you're the only one present. Not alone, necessarily,
but simply the only one present. It's good to ask,
and not demand an immediate answer. It's good

to ask the deepest, truest questions of yourself,
without insisting upon an immediate response.
It's good to ask, the way we might ask a misty
mountain waterfall, flowing over emerald rock,

covered in the shinny green moss of left alone aliveness.
Those truly wild shades of life, that need to remain largely
undiscovered — remote and hidden,

for the sake of something always worth preserving.
Life gushes forth in its infinite forms, and the best
we can do for ourselves, others, and the world we share,
is to take a full, unfettered moment to really notice.

We're all part of the great cascade of colorfully over flowing
    effervescence.
Life is always and forever over-lapping — layer upon layer of color,
light, texture, joy, and beauty —

exuberance rushing through, up, over, under, and upon itself.
There is a river, an ocean, and a reflecting pool,
in the center of each and every one of us…
a pristine wilderness, rainforest, and barren desert as well.

There is a waterfall rushing forth, flowing over the shinny
green moss of our own true aliveness. Life is always
over lapping — layer upon layer of luminous expression,
the gloaming of our natural transparency,
at the elemental point of our perception, including the

wasted, neglected, and thrown away days, that we
spend years attempting to get back. And what good
does it do, to hold our awareness on what we may

have squandered years ago? We can only live the life
that we've been given in the present. Life gushes forth
in its infinite forms, and it's pointless for us – utterly frivolous,

to attempt the construction of superfluous dams to try and stop it.
We only damn ourselves, with our wasted efforts.
Life gushes forth, like a healthy, playful child's imagination –

like those sounds that butterflies make on their maiden voyage,
while mist continues to rise from hidden waterfalls.

What do I want? I asked myself, near the beginning.
And my heart just sang me the answer; I want this!

Fresh Light & the Voices of Antiquity

I see giraffe, above the flame, beyond
the border, four feet to the left of daylight.

A family of giraffe, dancing to the delightful
sounds of Pachcebel, while two, less cheerful
crows do the dance of battle for position,
upon a single branch of a century-old Mimosa tree.

Sound echoing from the ancient archives,
as the day begins, adding
new light to the silent, vibrant history.

And eight paces to my right – zebra
standing still as a painted portrait of
heaven – quiet as the keys of a dusty piano.

Black and white supported on four legs,
like an animal keyboard, tuned to the
sacred sounds of mother Africa – grasslands

and open plains, red earth, stained for centuries,
with the blood of more than 50-millian species.

The stain of hunger, survival, power,
and human greed – the echoes
of more than a billion final breathes.

Hunger and the steady need to hunt,
fresh blood added to ancient soil,
the consumption
of meat for the sake of another day.

And in the center – blue as our illusion
of forever – empty as most promises of paradise.

And if we do good, we will live and we will die.
And if we do less than good, we will live and
we will die.

Pay very close attention to the day at hand,
or rather the moment, since that's all we ever really have.

Pay close attention to everything around you –
taste it, touch it, see it, smell it…
take it all in, as if there is no tomorrow.

Take it all in, and say what's in
your heart while it's still beating.

Don't wait for ghosts to say
it for you, when you're gone.

Pay close attention to the shimmering
dance of the living – where ecstatic
possibilities do their steady movements.

The natural in and out of essentially
everything – the fundamental,
quintessential, sacred breath of life.

The mystical night – the passion of stars
making love to the pulsating illusion of nothing but darkness…

And the dance goes on – the hunt continues –
hunger and feasting, new sounds, fresh light,
the voices of our time, blended with the voices of antiquity.

Myths and Artists

It's raining now, and I seem to have
lost Osiris. He left in a huff, when I
told him he wasn't qualified to weigh
my heart, or
accurately measure the merits of my work.

And where did I leave those waxy wings,
gifted to me by that cleaver daddy Daedelus?

The ones that my dear brother Icarus,
has no further earthly use for.
Did I leave them out in the rain yesterday?
And in this scorching heat of today?

Did the wax all melt in the open sun,
dripping through the crack in my oblivion?
And if they did, then what can I rely
on now to get beyond this labyrinth?

Did I ever really need those wings at all?
Isn't true flight all about love and artful soaring?

Learning to glide on those currents of
light-filled imagination.
And for the record…let me be the first
to say that Andy Warhol was wrong!

Most people will live out their entire
life, without even one minute of fame.
And a fifteen minute allotment for
everyone, remains utterly out of the question.

And I see my friend and mentor, the great
Henry Miller nodding his head in agreement,
seated upon the broad winged back of Pegasus.

Then suddenly leaping from the back of that
grand old horse, at the chance of mounting Aphrodite.

While Mozart keeps his composure on the
sidelines, humming a sweet, quixotic rhapsody,
and watching sixty million scattered molecules
searching for that bull in the sky – molecules
that once belonged to Hemingway.

And the ghost of Silvia keeps coming back to
turn off the stove – whispering something about
her unfinished poetry, and how death gave her immortality.

Michelangelo was one of the first to arrive
at the invitation only artful gathering,
held at the sacred ivory bungalow,

wearing his painter's cloths, and looking
appalled, as he starred
up at the plain white rectangular ceiling…

Take me back to the Sistine chapel!
I need to fix the ceiling in the cathedral –
I need to make the hand of God, reaching
toward man, look more like the hand of a woman.

More like the vision I had as I woke in the
quarry, with the sun breaking through those
majestic clouds – the mother hand reaching

out from within the celestial womb,
fingers extended in every direction,
to touch the heart of every living thing.

That's the vision I wanted to honor
upon the ceiling of the Sistine chapel.
But the Vatican wouldn't allow me
to, even though I threatened to resign.

I must go back now; I need to make it right.

Then he shook his head and mumbled
something about Gods and myths
and artists – finished his wine, and

slipped out through the window to the
garden, just in time to see Persephone
slip back underground.

And the search continues; Demeter for
her daughter, bees for flowers, artists
for perfection, beauty, peace of mind.

Getting to the Point

It's getting to the point, in which I must
paint the portraits and visions I claim as
my own. Da Vinci's do nothing for me.

I could care less if I see the Mona Lisa
ever again. I'm quite content that it is in
Paris, behind bulletproof glass, and that

I am not. And I have no desire to join the
legions of frantic fiddlers, in their fruitless
attempts to figure out whether or not Leonardo

left some secret code behind. There's plenty of
mystery for all of us – enough to cover
the earth several times, hold all the stars,

rotate all the planets, fill black holes with
cosmic wonder, while managing all the known
and unknown galaxies. And still plenty

more after that. I'm simply not inspired
by church sanctioned paintings of infants
with haloes, forever deprived of their earthy
mothers plump and fertile breasts…

Give me O'Keeffe instead! She's all flower,
all bone, all mountain, all unbridled passion.
She is the over-sized imagination –
artfully unapologetic for her organic sensuality.

She lays it out, opens it up, then enlarges
her visions, so we need not deny what we see.
And no one seems to suspect O'Keeffe of
leaving us a secret code. She was raw,

unpretentious, extravagant only in her
simplicity – ostentatious in her full and
natural acceptance. She is all flower, all
bone, and all black abstraction intermittently –

all dry sand and endless desert. She is all Iris,
then earth-sized poppy. And as the sun
comes up, she becomes the ubiquitous birch
trees at dawn. Though she isn't the only
artist that I favor more than Da Vinci.
There have been drawings on my refrigerator
door, that touched my heart more deeply than
Da Vinci's superfluous depictions of the Madonna.

There are numerous known and unknown artists
that move me more. But what I'm getting at here
and now, today, at this point in time, is the urge I
have to paint some of the visions I claim as my own.

To lay some of the beauty I see, upon a canvas
tightly stretched across a wooden frame.
To lay it down, simply because I feel the urge to,
and because I know my artful urges are inspired

by the forces I know to be good. Though I will not
copy O'Keeffe, or make any attempt to imitate
Da Vinci, or the amazing Michelangelo for that

matter, even though I do love and admire his truly
astonishing works of art. I want to do with watercolors,
what I've managed to do with the arrangement of words.

I want to listen to the empty canvas, and converse
with it. Then permit the paint to fill it in, much the
same way the words show up, with their own
eagerness to dance across pale blue linear lines.

I want to honor my own intuition, with brushes
and paint – surrender to the visions that wish to
come through, then glance back at them near
the end of the day, and smile at what I laid down.

And when I trade in the labyrinth, one last time,
for some sweet loquacious lullaby, I will seek
no consolation for what I failed to leave behind.

I will have left 10,000 sonnets for the thirsty ones
to suckle and be nurtured by. Thousands of pages
to be taken in, interpreted, and converted into a
secret code, by those who need the mystery to shield
them from the pure and simple meaning of their own life.

And hopefully there will be those who see
and savor it for what it is…all flower, all bone,
all mountain, sprinkled heavily with genuine
diamond dust, and a well-rounded oz. of fools gold.

Closing Words to the Reader

Dear Reader,

I'm delighted that you've made your way to this page. You represent the fourth pillar of completion, with regard to this book. It needed first and foremost to be written, then edited, published, and now read by you.

You, having taken a poetic journey through these pages, complete this book in a way it could not be otherwise. The reader represents a vital part of the creative process, and I am grateful to you for the pivotal role that you play.

Thank you for taking in what I needed to express – for letting in what I needed to lay down. I hope the essence of all these poetic words and phrases stay with you as long as you want them to. And I hope you will want them to for many wonderful years to come.

I have for that reason included a blank page opposite this one for you to fill in with your own words, if you choose to. Any words that feel true for you will be perfect. They will complete this book in a whole new way, and allow our words – yours and mine, to be companions. And in the spirit of artful companionship, I thank you now for whatever you're willing to write.

May all your brightest dreams be fully realized.

Wayne Allen LeVine

More From Wayne Allen LeVine

"Throughout the ages, people of great wisdom have said that the only true vocation comes from one's ability to look in, and create our gifts to the world from what they see. Wayne Allen LeVine is in love with life. His great enthusiasm is contagious."

> – Stellasue Lee
> Poetry Editor, Rattle

The poetry of Wayne Allen LeVine speaks to the romantic soul in all of us. You can read more unique and spiritually lifting poetry in his other book "Forgiveness for Forgotten Dreams" found online and in most major bookstores.

Or you can contact the publisher and order this book direct for $13.95 plus $3.50 shipping at:

The Center Press
P.O. Box 6936
Thousand Oaks, CA 91360-6936
(818) 889-7071   FAX (818) 889-7072
www.centerbooks.com
email: center@centerbooks.com

Forgiveness for Forgotten Dreams
by Wayne Allen LeVine
ISBN 1-889198-10-2